THE CHOCOLATE BOX

Candies & Desserts

Joanna Farrow

RIZZOLI
NEW YORK

First published in the United States of America in 1995 by
RIZZOLI INTERNATIONAL PUBLICATIONS, INC.
300 Park Avenue South, New York, NY 10010

First published in the United Kingdom in 1994 by
HARLAXTON PUBLISHING LIMITED
A Member of the Weldon International Group of Companies

Copyright © 1994 : Harlaxton Publishing Limited
Design copyright © 1994 : Harlaxton Publishing Limited

Library of Congress Cataloguing-in-Publication Data
Farrow, Joanna
Chocolate Box/Joanna Farrow
p.   cm.
Includes indexes.
Contents: [1] Cakes & Cookies - - [2] Confectionery & Desserts.
ISBN : 0-8478-1869-1 (set) .
1. Cookery (Chocolate) 2. Desserts. I. Title.
TX767.C5F39 1995
641.6'374 - - dc20   94-43379 CIP

Publisher: Robin Burgess
Publishing Manager & Design: Rachel Rush
Editor: Alison Leach
Illustrator: Lyne Breeze, Linden Artists
Photographer: James Duncan
Home Economist: Sue Maggs
Stylist: Madelaine Brehaut
Typesetter: John Macauley, Seller's
Color separation: GA Graphics
Printer: Imago , Singapore

Contents

The wonderful versatility of chocolate needs little introduction, and whether you are looking for a simple everyday dessert or an extravagant confection for a dinner party you will find many delicious chocolate treats in this book.

The desserts chapters include some good old favorites such as Steamed Chocolate Pudding with Apple and Raisin Topping (p.35) and Profiteroles with Glossy Chocolate Sauce (p.46) as well as some more unusual ideas. There are also 'freeze ahead' desserts which are especially useful at times when you have plenty of other cooking to do as they can of course be made well in advance.

Opposite: Decorative chocolate ideas.

The texture of chocolate lends itself to numerous decorations, whether melted and piped or just prettily shaped. The following ideas apply to special desserts, although some of the decorations can equally well be used on ice creams, mousses, and chilled or frozen desserts.

Once made, chocolate decorations will keep in a cool, dry place for a couple of weeks. Interleave them with baking parchment to prevent sticking.

Chocolate Chips

Use dark, milk, or white chocolate at room temperature. Using a sharp knife, cut the chocolate into very small pieces and scatter over chilled or frozen desserts.

Chocolate Cup Shells

These are used as containers for the Chocolate Colettes (p.22). Alternatively, use them as candy cases for dipped fruits, or other small chocolates.

Melt a little dark, milk, or white chocolate (you will need about 4 oz/4 squares to make 20 shells). Using the back of a teaspoon, spread a little chocolate over the base and sides of foil or paper candy cases. Invert on a sheet of baking parchment and leave in a cool place or chill until set. Peel the foil or paper carefully from the chocolate.

Chocolate Leaves

Use non-poisonous, well-defined, pretty leaves such as rose, mint, lemon balm, scented geranium, bay, or holly. They must be in good condition, clean, and dried thoroughly to work successfully.

Melt a little dark, milk, or white chocolate (you will need approximately 2 oz/2 squares to cover 10 leaves, depending on their size). Using a paintbrush, paint the underside of the leaves with a thick layer of chocolate. Avoid letting the chocolate run over the edges of the leaf as this would make it difficult to peel away the leaf. Leave in a cool place or chill until set; then peel the leaf away carefully from the chocolate.

If the chocolate layer is too thin, apply a second coat before peeling away the leaf.

Dipped Fruits

Fruits such as strawberries, grapes, gooseberries, and cherries look very attractive dipped in chocolate, whether as a decoration, or to serve with coffee after a dinner party.

Melt a little dark, milk, or white chocolate (you will need about 2 oz/2 squares chocolate to coat 15 fruits). Half-dip the fruits, one at a time into the chocolate; then let the excess fall back into the bowl. Transfer the fruits to a sheet of baking parchment and leave to set.

Feathered Chocolate Pieces

Melt 3 oz/3 squares dark or milk chocolate. Melt 1 oz/ 1 square white chocolate separately. Spread the dark or milk chocolate on to a piece of baking parchment. While it is still runny, use a teaspoon to drizzle the white chocolate over it. Run the tip of a toothpick or metal skewer through the chocolate to give a feathered finish. Chill until set. Peel away the paper and break the chocolate into irregular pieces.

Piped Chocolate Shapes

Melt a little dark, milk, or white chocolate and place in a pastry bag fitted with a writing tip. Alternatively, use a paper pastry bag and cut off the merest tip. Pipe small shapes on to a sheet of baking parchment. (Do not make them too big or sprawling as they will be difficult to use.)

Leave in a cool place, or chill until set. Peel the paper away carefully from the chocolate and use the shapes to decorate a chilled or frozen dessert.

Run-Out Chocolate Leaves

Trace the outline of small attractive leaves (ivy looks particularly good) on to baking parchment. Melt a little dark, milk, or white chocolate (you will need about 3 oz/ 3 squares to make 10 leaves). Place a quarter in a pastry bag fitted with a small writing tip. (Alternatively, use a paper pastry bag and cut off the merest tip.) Use the chocolate to pipe over the traced outline; then chill for 5 minutes. Using a small teaspoon or paintbrush, fill the center of the shapes with the remaining melted chocolate. Leave in a cool place or chill until set. Peel the paper away carefully from the chocolate.

Home-made candies illustrates chocolate in its most luxurious form. Not only are home-made candies perfect for adding the finishing touch to a special occasion dessert, it will also be greeted with delight when served with coffee at a dinner party.

Young chocolate lovers are not left out of the fun – there are pretty chocolate mice and colorful chocolate lollipops, made at a fraction of the price of bought versions.

Most of the chocolates can be made up to a week in advance, provided that they are stored in a cool place. Those including cream will keep for two to three days.

After-Dinner Mints

Makes 25

¾ cup pastel dinner mints
4 oz/4 squares milk chocolate
4 oz/4 squares dark or semisweet chocolate

Draw a 10x5 inch rectangle on a sheet of baking parchment. Place the mints in a double-thickness plastic bag and crush with a rolling pin until virtually powdered.

Break the milk chocolate into pieces and melt in a heatproof bowl over a saucepan of simmering water. Remove from the heat and stir in the crushed mints. Spread on the parchment, just over the edges of the marked rectangle. Leave to set.

Melt the dark or semisweet chocolate as above and spread quickly over the milk chocolate. Leave to set. Using a sharp knife, cut the chocolate into 2x1 inch rectangles. Keep in a cool place until ready to serve.

Cook's Tip

Take care that the milk chocolate has set completely before spreading with the dark. The dark chocolate needs to be spread fairly quickly so that it does not melt into the milk.

Previous page:
Chocolate after dinner-selection, left to right, After-Dinner Mints, Brandied Chocolate Cherries, and Chocolate Praline Squares.

Chocolate Praline Squares

Makes 28

2 oz/¼ cup superfine sugar
2 oz/½ cup blanched almonds, roughly chopped
7 oz/7 squares milk chocolate
3 fl oz/5 tablespoons heavy cream
½ teaspoon vanilla extract
3 oz/3 squares dark chocolate

Oil a baking sheet lightly. Place the sugar in a small, heavy-based saucepan with 3 tablespoons water. Heat gently until the sugar dissolves, then bring to the boil and boil until the sugar turns golden. Stir in the almonds and pour onto the oiled baking sheet. Leave to harden.

When brittle, place the mixture in a double-thickness plastic bag and beat the praline with a rolling pin until finely crushed.

Break the milk chocolate into pieces and place in a small saucepan with the cream and vanilla extract. Heat gently, stirring until smooth. Remove from the heat and leave to cool completely.

Moisten a 1 pint/2½ cup loaf pan and line with baking parchment. Beat the praline into the chocolate mixture and pour into the pan. Level the surface and chill until firm.

Break the dark chocolate into pieces and melt in a heatproof bowl over a pan of simmering water. Invert the milk chocolate slab on to the work surface. Spread half the dark chocolate over one side of the slab. Leave for a few minutes to harden, then turn the slab over and spread with the remaining dark chocolate.

Chill until firm; then cut into 28 squares.

Brandied Chocolate Cherries

Makes 24

24 ripe cherries
2 tablespoons brandy
4 oz/4 squares dark or semisweet chocolate

Pit the cherries using a stoner or knife, keeping the stalks intact if possible. Place the cherries in a small bowl and add the brandy. Cover and leave to soak overnight in a cool place.

Break the chocolate into pieces and melt in a heatproof bowl over a saucepan of simmering water. Drain the cherries and dry on paper towels. Line a baking sheet with baking parchment.

Dip the cherries in the melted chocolate and transfer to the paper. Leave to set and serve in foil candy cases.

Variation
Use rum, amaretto, or kirsch instead of the brandy.

Chocolate Mice

Makes 8

5 oz/5 squares dark or milk chocolate
5 oz/5 squares white chocolate
A little pink paste food coloring
1 licorice shoestring
1 strawberry shoestring

Polish eight chocolate mice molds with cotton wool. (If you have fewer molds, make the dark and light mice in two batches.)

Break the dark or milk chocolate into pieces and melt in a heatproof bowl over a saucepan of simmering water. Melt the white chocolate separately. Reserve a table-spoonful of the white chocolate and stir a dot of food coloring into the remainder. Spoon into half the molds and tap gently to remove any air bubbles. Cut the strawberry shoestring into four 3 inch lengths and push into place for tails. Turn the dark or milk chocolate into the remaining molds, using the licorice shoestring for the tails. Chill the molds for 30 minutes or until set.

Invert the molds on the work surface and tap to remove the mice. Using a fine paintbrush, paint the reserved white chocolate on the mice for eyes and noses.

Cook's Tip

Chocolate mice molds are most widely available from department stores and kitchen shops. You will find them in specialist cake decorating shops throughout the year. When coloring the white chocolate, make sure you use a paste rather than liquid coloring which would make the chocolate seize. Alternatively, leave the mice white – they will look just as effective.

Chocolate Lollipops

Makes 8

1 oz sugarpaste
Red food coloring
6 oz/6 squares milk chocolate
8 strawberry shoestrings
M & Ms
1 oz/1 square dark chocolate

Draw eight 2½ inch circles, spaced slightly apart on baking parchment. Turn the paper over and lay on a baking sheet or tray. Arrange eight popsicle sticks with the ends 1 inch inside each circle. Color the sugarpaste red and shape 8 round noses and 8 mouths.

Break the milk chocolate into pieces and melt in a heat-proof bowl over a saucepan of simmering water. Divide among the circles, spreading it out to the edges and being careful not to dislodge the sticks.

While the chocolate is still soft, press the noses and mouths into position. Add M&Ms for eyes. Crumple up the shoestrings and position for hair.

Melt the dark chocolate and use to decorate the eyes with a small paintbrush. Leave to set.

Left: Chocolate fun ideas for children, Chocolate Mice and Chocolate Lollipops.

13

Chocolate-Dipped Fudge

Makes 1½ lb

1 lb/2 cups granulated sugar
3 oz/⅓ cup unsalted butter
¼ pint/⅔ cup milk
6 oz can evaporated milk
2 teaspoons vanilla extract
3 oz/3 squares dark, milk, or white chocolate to decorate

Oil a 7 inch shallow square baking pan lightly. Place the sugar, butter, milk, and evaporated milk in a large, heavy-based saucepan and heat gently until the butter has melted and sugar has dissolved.

Bring to the boil and boil without stirring until a temperature of 240°F is reached on a candy thermometer. (Alternatively, drop a little of the mixture into a bowl of iced water. It should form a soft ball when rolled between the fingers.)

Remove from the heat and add the vanilla extract. Beat with a wooden spoon until the mixture is thick and slightly grainy in texture. Scrape into the prepared pan and level the surface. Leave to cool.

Cut the fudge into small squares and remove from the pan. Transfer to a sheet of baking parchment, spaced slightly apart, and leave to dry out for 1–2 hours.

Break the chocolate into pieces and melt in a heatproof bowl over a pan of simmering water. Half-dip each piece of fudge in the chocolate, letting the excess drop back into the bowl. Return to the baking parchment to set.

Right: Chocolate gifts, left to right, Chocolate Fudge, Fresh Cream Truffles, and Chocolate Orange Logs.

Fresh Cream Truffles

Makes about 24   4 oz/4 squares dark chocolate
4 oz/4 squares milk chocolate
4 fl oz/½ cup heavy cream
2 tablespoons Cointreau or Grand Marnier
Finely grated rind of 1 orange

To Decorate: 4 oz/4 squares dark chocolate
4 oz/4 squares white chocolate

Break the dark and milk chocolate into pieces and melt together with the cream in a heavy-based saucepan. Remove from the heat and stir in the liqueur, and orange rind until smooth. Chill until fairly firm.

Using a teaspoon, take scoops of the mixture and roll these into small balls. Chill again until firm.

To decorate, melt the remaining dark and white chocolate in separate bowls. Dip half the truffles, one at a time, in the dark chocolate until coated. Transfer to a baking parchment-lined baking sheet. Touch the surface of each with the back of a fork for a textured finish. Repeat with the white chocolate. Chill for up to 3 days before serving.

Variations

* Use rum or brandy instead of the orange-flavored liqueur and omit the orange rind.
* Instead of coating in melted chocolate, roll the truffles in cocoa powder or finely chopped, toasted nuts.

Chocolate Orange Logs

Makes about 30

2 oz amaretto cookies
4 oz/4 squares dark chocolate
3 fl oz/5 tablespoons heavy cream
Finely grated rind of ½ orange
1 tablespoon Cointreau or orange-flavored liqueur
Cocoa powder for dusting

To Decorate:

2 oz/2 squares dark chocolate
Cocoa powder and confectioners' sugar for dusting

Place the amaretto cookies in a strong plastic bag and crush finely. Break the chocolate into pieces and melt it in a heatproof bowl over a saucepan of simmering water. Stir in the cream, orange rind, liqueur, and crushed cookies, and stir until evenly combined.

Using hands dusted with cocoa powder, halve the mixture and shape into two logs, each about ½ inch wide. Chill until firm.

Break the remaining chocolate into pieces and melt it as above. Brush over the logs and then cut widthways into 1 inch lengths. Serve the portions dusted with cocoa powder and confectioners' sugar.

Double-Dipped Fruits

Makes about 30   30 small fruits such as
cape gooseberries, cherries, strawberries,
or seedless black or white grapes
2 oz/2 squares dark chocolate
2 oz/2 squares white chocolate

Pull back the stems from the the cape gooseberries but leave attached. Leave the stems on the cherries or strawberries. Separate the grapes. Break the dark chocolate into pieces and melt in a heatproof bowl over a saucepan of simmering water. Melt the white chocolate separately.

Line a large baking sheet or tray with baking parchment. Half-dip the fruits in the white chocolate and place on the paper. Chill for several minutes until beginning to set; dip the fruits again in the dark chocolate, adjusting the angle so that some of the white chocolate still shows. Keep in a cool place until ready to serve.

Cook's Tip
Larger fruits such as wedges of peach, nectarine, apricot, or mango look pretty drizzled with melted chocolate. Lay the wedges on parchment paper. Place the chocolate in a paper pastry bag; snip off the end and "scribble" the chocolate over the fruits.

Left: Double Dipped Fruits.

Checkered Chocolate Marzipan

Makes 11 oz

8 oz white almond paste
Pink or green food coloring
Confectioners' sugar for dusting
3 oz/3 squares dark or semisweet chocolate

Divide the almond paste in half and knead a little pink or green food coloring into one half. Form each half into a 4x1x1 inch block. On a surface lightly dusted with confectioners' sugar, cut each block lengthways into nine even-sized rectangles. Re-assemble the rectangles into two large blocks, alternating the colors on each to make a checkered pattern. Trim the edges to neaten if necessary.

Break the chocolate into pieces and melt in a heatproof bowl over a saucepan of simmering water. Place the rectangles of almond paste on a sheet of baking parchment. Spread a little melted chocolate along one long side of each and chill briefly until completely set. Turn the paste so that the chocolate-coated sides are underneath, then coat the remaining sides with chocolate. Chill until set; then cut widthways into slices.

Cook's Tip

If the rectangles of almond paste do not stick together easily, brush with a little water or melted apricot jam before assembling.

Coconut Kisses

Makes about 24

8 oz confectioners' sugar
2 oz/¼ cup unsalted butter, softened
3½ oz/1¼ cups shredded coconut
Few drops of pink food coloring

4 oz/4 squares dark or milk chocolate to decorate

Sift the confectioners' sugar into a heatproof bowl. Add the butter and 2 tablespoons hot water. Rest the bowl over a pan of simmering water and beat until the mixture is warm and runny. Add the coconut and stir the mixture until combined.

Transfer half the mixture to a separate bowl and beat in a little pink food coloring. Shape both mixtures into small oval shapes about 1¼ inches long and transfer to a baking parchment-lined baking sheet. Chill until firm.

Break the chocolate into pieces and melt in a heatproof bowl over a pan of simmering water. Place a quarter of the chocolate in a paper pastry bag and snip off the tip.

Drizzle the chocolate over half the sweets. Half-dip the remaining coconut shapes, one at a time, in the remaining melted chocolate, letting the excess chocolate drop back into the bowl; then return the shapes to the baking sheet. Leave to set.

Left: Coconut Kisses.

Chocolate-Coated Peanut Brittle

Makes 11oz

6 oz/1½ cups shelled, raw peanuts
8 oz/1 cup granulated sugar
4 oz/⅔ cup light brown sugar
2 oz light corn syrup
1 oz /3 tablespoons unsalted butter
¼ teaspoon baking soda
4 oz/4 squares dark or milk chocolate

Oil an 11x8 inch shallow baking pan lightly and line with non-stick baking parchment. Grease the paper lightly. Toast the peanuts.

Put the granulated and brown sugars in a saucepan with the syrup and 4 tablespoons water. Heat gently until the sugar has dissolved. Bring to the boil and boil rapidly until the temperature reaches 310°F on a candy thermometer. (Alternatively, drop a little of the syrup into a bowl of iced water. It should form hard and brittle threads.)

Remove from the heat and dip the base of the pan in cold water to prevent further cooking. Stir in the butter, baking soda and toasted peanuts immediately. Pour the mixture into the baking pan and leave for several hours until brittle.

Break the chocolate into pieces and melt in a heatproof bowl over a saucepan of simmering water. Remove the peanut brittle from the pan and place on a sheet of baking parchment. Spread half the chocolate over the brittle and chill until beginning to set. Turn the brittle over and spread with the remaining chocolate. Leave until set. To break the brittle into chunks, use a sturdy knife, tapping with the end of a rolling pin.

Cook's Tip

Wrap the peanut brittle in a plastic bag or cellophane, or store in a lidded jar as the brittle turns sticky when left exposed.

Rocky Roads

Makes about 1 lb

6 white marshmallows
6 pink marshmallows
2 oz/⅓ cup blanched almonds, chopped
1 oz/3 tablespoons raisins
8 oz/8 squares milk chocolate
2 oz/½ cup slivered almonds, toasted

Using scissors, snip the marshmallows into small pieces. Mix the chopped almonds with the marshmallows and the raisins.

Break 6 oz/6 squares of the chocolate into pieces and melt in a heatproof bowl over a pan of simmering water. Add to the marshmallow mixture and stir until combined. Transfer to a piece of baking parchment. Wrap the paper around the mixture, pressing it into a roll, about 1¼ inches thick. Chill until firm.

Melt the remaining chocolate as above. Scatter the slivered almonds over another piece of baking parchment. Spread the chocolate roll with the melted chocolate, then coat in the slivered almonds. Chill briefly until firm. Cut the roll widthways into slices.

Left: Chocolate-Coated Peanut Brittle and Rocky Roads.

Mini Chocolate Tuiles

Makes about 28

1 oz/2 tablespoons unsalted butter
3 egg whites
3½ oz/scant ½ cup superfine sugar
2 tablespoons all-purpose flour
1 tablespoon cocoa powder
½ teaspoon ground mixed spice (apple pie spice)
2 tablespoons heavy cream
Confectioners' sugar and cocoa powder for dusting

Line a large baking sheet with non-stick baking parchment. Melt the butter and leave to cool slightly.

Place the egg whites and the sugar in a bowl and whisk lightly. Sift the flour, cocoa powder, and the mixed spice into the bowl. Add the cream and melted butter, and beat until smooth.

Place teaspoonfuls of the mixture on the baking sheet, spaced well apart and spread out slightly. (You will need to bake 10 at a time.) Bake in a preheated oven at 350°F for 6-8 minutes until the edges are slightly darker in color. Remove from the oven and leave for 1 minute before lifting the cookies over a rolling pin and leaving to set into crisp, curled shapes. Repeat with the remaining mixture.

Store in an airtight container and serve dusted with confectioners' sugar and cocoa powder.

Cook's Tip

If the tuiles cool on the baking sheet before you have had time to shape them, return them to the oven for a few moments to soften and then try again.

Chocolate Colettes

Makes 24

5 oz/5 squares dark chocolate

Filling:

3 oz/¾ cup pistachio nuts
6 oz/6 squares dark chocolate
4 fl oz/½ cup heavy cream
2 tablespoons amaretto liqueur or brandy

Break the dark chocolate into pieces and melt in a heatproof bowl over a saucepan of simmering water. Spoon inside 24 foil candy cases, spreading evenly up the sides. Invert the cases on a baking parchment-lined tray or baking sheet and chill until set.

Chocolate Walnut Fudge

Makes 1¼ lb   4 oz/4 squares dark chocolate, grated
2 oz/½ cup broken walnuts, finely chopped
1 lb/2 cups granulated sugar
2 oz/¼ cup unsalted butter
3 fl oz/5 tablespoons evaporated milk

Oil a 7 inch shallow square baking pan lightly. Place the sugar, butter, and evaporated milk in a large, heavy-based saucepan and heat gently until the butter has dissolved and the sugar has melted. Bring to the boil and boil without stirring until a temperature of 240°F is reached on a candy thermometer. (Alternatively, drop a little of the mixture into a bowl of iced water. It should form a soft ball when rolled between the fingers.)

Remove from the heat and leave for 2 minutes. Add the grated chocolate and walnuts, and beat with a wooden spoon until the mixture is slightly grainy. Scrape into the prepared pan and level the surface. Leave to cool.

Cut the fudge into small squares and remove from the pan. Transfer to a sheet of baking parchment, spaced just slightly apart, and leave to dry out.

Variation
Add 2 tablespoons brandy, rum, or orange liqueur to the fudge when beating in the chocolate.

Put the pistachio nuts in a heatproof bowl and cover with boiling water. Leave for 1 minute. Drain the nuts and rub between several sheets of paper towels to remove the skins. Reserve 24 of the best nuts and chop roughly.

Break the remaining chocolate into pieces. Bring the cream just to the boil in a saucepan. Remove from the heat and stir in the chocolate until it has melted. Spoon into a bowl and stir in the liqueur or brandy. Leave to cool and then beat until peaking softly. Place in a pastry bag fitted with a star tip.

Pipe a little of the mixture into the chocolate cases and sprinkle with the whole pistachio nuts. Use the remaining mixture to pipe swirls on to each. Decorate with the reserved whole pistachio nuts.

Above: Chocolate Colettes in pretty candy cases.

Next page: Chocolate Egg Selection, beautifully decorated to make perfect Easter gifts.

White Chocolate Clusters

Makes 7 oz

4 oz/4 squares white chocolate
2 oz/½ cup unsalted peanuts, hazelnuts,
or Brazil nuts, roughly chopped
1 oz/3 tablespoons raisins

Break the chocolate into pieces and melt in a heatproof bowl over a saucepan of simmering water. Mix the nuts with the raisins and add to the chocolate, stirring very lightly until just coated in chocolate.

Line a baking sheet with baking parchment. Place teaspoonfuls of the chocolate mixture on the paper and leave to set. Serve in small paper cases.

Home-made Easter Eggs

A great variety of Easter egg molds are available from either specialist cake decorating or kitchen equipment shops. There are many different ways of decorating the eggs. They can be made using one type of chocolate or using two or three different ones. As a guide allow about 2 oz/2 squares chocolate for a 2½ inch egg, 6 oz/6 squares chocolate for a 4½ inch egg and 8 oz/8 squares chocolate for a 5-6 inch egg.

Wash and dry the molds thoroughly, and then polish the insides with a little cotton wool.

Break the chocolate into pieces and melt in a heatproof bowl over a saucepan of simmering water. Spoon into the two half molds, spreading up the sides with the back of a teaspoon. Place, face-down, on a sheet of baking parchment and chill for 30 minutes. Spread with a second layer of chocolate and chill until set.

To remove from the molds, carefully ease the sides of the mold away from the chocolate. Invert the mold on a work surface and tap firmly to release the chocolate. If the chocolate will not part from the mold, freeze for several minutes so that the chocolate contracts slightly.

To assemble an egg, lay one half on a cup or ramekin and brush the edges generously with a little more melted chocolate. Press the second half gently into position.

Cook's Tip

Try to work with cool hands, if necessary putting them in cold water for several minutes. When releasing the chocolate from the molds, support the molds in a dish towel so that the warmth from your hands does not dull the chocolate.

Variations

Filigree Eggs – Place a little white chocolate in a paper pastry bag and snip off the tip. Drizzle wavy lines into each half of the mold. Chill for 5 minutes; then spread with the dark or milk chocolate quite quickly as the warmth of the chocolate will soften the piped white chocolate. Chill and unmold as above. As a variation use dark or milk chocolate for piping and white chocolate for spreading.

Latticed Eggs – Make as for filigree eggs; piping the white chocolate in a lattice pattern.

Polka Dot Eggs – Make as for filigree eggs; piping dots of white chocolate into the molds.

Decorating Easter Eggs

Once the Easter egg shells are made, there are various ways to decorate them prettily for presentation, from simple ribbon ties to detailed piping.

Ribbon Eggs – Place the egg in a ramekin or small dish to steady it. Place a dot of melted chocolate at the base and top of the egg over the join. Secure a piece of ribbon over the melted chocolate, covering the join around the shell. If liked, add a second ribbon around the "waist" of the egg and finish with a small bow.

Shell Borders – For either one large or two small eggs, bring 4 tablespoons heavy cream to the boil in a small pan. Stir in 2 oz/2 squares broken dark or milk chocolate until it has melted. Leave to cool; then beat until the mixture forms soft peaks. Place in a pastry bag fitted with a shell or star tip. Place the egg in a ramekin or small dish to steady it and pipe a row of shells over the join.

Dots and Dashes – Place the egg in a ramekin or small dish to steady it. Melt a little dark, milk, or white chocolate and place this in a pastry bag fitted with a fine writing tip. (Alternatively, use a paper pastry bag and snip off the merest tip.) Pipe clusters of dots or scribbled lines of chocolate over one half of the shell. Chill the egg for 5 minutes until the piping has set; then turn the shell over carefully and repeat on the other side.

Wrapping Easter Eggs

After the eggs are decorated and any applied piping has hardened, they can be arranged attractively in boxes or cellophane. Cut circles or squares of cellophane and use to enclose the eggs, tying the ends with lengths of ribbon. If using boxes, cover them with wrapping paper and line with crumpled tissue paper. Bought, decorated gift boxes or bags can also be used. Again, line them with crumpled tissue paper to cushion and enhance the egg.

This chapter contains a delicious selection of both old favorites and more unusual recipes, either to serve as a simple mid-week dessert or to grace a more elaborate dinner.

Mouthwatering hot chocolate sponges like the Steamed Chocolate Pudding with Apple and Raisin Topping (p.35) and the Chocolate Pudding Pie (this page) make perfect winter warmers. Pastry lovers can indulge in a Chocolate Meringue Pie (p.40), a rich Chocolate Walnut Pie (p.42) or an interesting variation on a flaky Almond and Chocolate Pithiviers (p.41) with an irresistible layer of chocolate sauce. Whatever your choice, do not forget to serve with plenty of pouring cream for the ultimate indulgence!

Chocolate Pudding Pie

Serves 5

4 oz/½ cup unsalted butter, softened
8 oz/1¼ cups light brown sugar
1 teaspoon vanilla extract
2 eggs, beaten
4 oz/1 cup self-raising flour
4 tablespoons cocoa powder
Milk
Confectioners' sugar for dusting

Grease a 2½ pint/6¼ cup pie dish lightly. Beat the butter and 4 oz/⅔ cup of the sugar with the vanilla until light and fluffy. Beat in the eggs gradually, a little at a time until light and fluffy, adding a little of the flour to prevent curdling. Sift the remaining flour with 2 tablespoons of the cocoa powder and fold into the egg mixture. Add a little milk to mix to a soft, dropping consistency.

Beat the remaining sugar in a bowl with the remaining cocoa powder and 8 fl oz/1 cup hot water. Pour over the mixture in the pie dish. Bake in a preheated oven at 375°F for about 35 minutes until slightly risen. Dust with confectioners' sugar and serve hot with cream or ice cream.

Cook's Tip

This delicious pudding separates during cooking, giving a spongy topping and a smooth chocolate sauce in the base. Avoid over-cooking as the mixture will dry out.

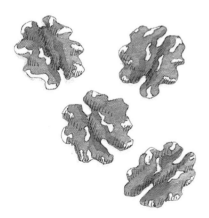

Previous page: Steamed Chocolate Pudding with Apple and Raisin Topping (p.35).

Chocolate Crêpes with Almonds and Peaches

Serves 4

Crêpes: 3½ oz/1 cup less 2 tablespoons all-purpose flour
2 tablespoons cocoa powder
1 tablespoon superfine sugar
1 egg
½ pint/1¼ cups milk
Oil for frying

Filling: 4 oz white almond paste
1 oz/¼ cup slivered almonds
4 small ripe peaches, or 8 canned peach halves

Sauce: 5 oz/5 squares dark chocolate
¼ pint/⅔ cup heavy cream

To make the crêpes, sift the flour and cocoa powder into a bowl. Stir in the sugar. Make a well in the center and add the egg with a little of the milk. Whisk the egg and the milk together, incorporating the flour gradually to make a smooth paste. Whisk in the remaining milk to make a creamy smooth batter.

Heat a little oil in a medium frying pan. Drain off the oil and pour in a little of the batter. Tilt the pan so that the batter coats the base of the pan; then cook over a moderate heat until set and golden on the underside. Flip the crêpe over with a spatula and cook until golden. Remove from the pan and add a little more oil. Make seven more crêpes in the same way.

To make the filling, grate the almond paste and toast the almonds lightly. Halve and pit the peaches. Arrange a peach half towards one side of a crêpe and sprinkle with about an eighth of the grated almond paste. Fold over the other side of the crêpe to enclose and then roll up into a cone. Place on a large, lightly oiled baking sheet. Fill the remaining crêpes in the same way.

Bake the crêpes in a preheated oven at 350°F for about 10 minutes until warmed through. Meanwhile, make the sauce. Break the chocolate into pieces. Bring the cream to the boil in a small saucepan; stir in the chocolate until it has melted. Transfer the crêpes to serving plates and pour over a little sauce. Serve sprinkled with the toasted nuts.

Cook's Tip

For convenience, the crêpes can be made in advance. Stack between squares of baking parchment to prevent them from sticking together and store in a plastic bag in the refrigerator. They also freeze very well, ready for an easy assembly.

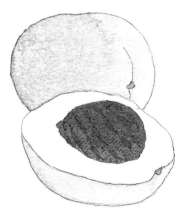

Hot Chocolate Soufflés

Serves 6

3 oz/3 squares dark chocolate
2 oz/¼ cup unsalted butter
1½ oz/⅓ cup all-purpose flour
¼ teaspoon ground ginger
½ pint/1¼ cups milk
5 eggs, separated
1 oz/2½ tablespoons superfine sugar
Confectioners' sugar for dusting

Grease six individual soufflé dishes. Break the chocolate into pieces. Melt the butter in a large saucepan. Add the flour and ginger and cook, stirring, for 1 minute. Blend in the milk gradually until the mixture is smooth. Bring to the boil and cook, stirring, for 1 minute until thickened. Beat in the chocolate until it has melted. Add the egg yolks.

Beat the egg whites in a large bowl until stiff. Beat in the sugar gradually. Using a large metal spoon, fold a quarter of the egg whites into the chocolate mixture; then fold in the remaining egg whites carefully. Turn into the prepared dishes, filling each one almost to the top. Place on a baking sheet and bake in a preheated oven at 375°F for about 20 minutes until well risen and just firm to the touch. Serve immediately, dusted with confectioners' sugar.

Variations

For additional flavor, add 2 tablespoons brandy or rum, or 2 tablespoons very strong dark coffee when making the sauce. If you do not have individual soufflé dishes, use a large 2½ pint/6 ¼ cup greased dish and allow an extra 20–25 minutes cooking time.

Chocolate and Raspberry Torte

Serves 6

5 oz/⅔ cup unsalted butter, softened
5 oz/generous ¾ cup light brown sugar
5 oz/1¼ cups ground almonds
4½ oz/1 cup plus 2 tablespoons self-raising flour
2 tablespoons cocoa powder
1 egg
8 oz/1½ cups fresh or frozen raspberries
2 tablespoons slivered almonds
Confectioners' sugar for dusting

Grease an 8 inch spring form cake pan. Beat the butter and sugar together until lightly creamed. Add the ground almonds, flour, cocoa powder, and egg, then beat until evenly combined. Press half the mixture into the prepared pan and flatten lightly.

Scatter with the raspberries to within ½ inch of the edges. Sprinkle with the remaining mixture and top with the almonds. Bake in a preheated oven at 350°F for 40-50 minutes until slightly risen.

Cool in the pan for 10 minutes; then dust with confectioners' sugar. Serve warm or cold with cream.

Cook's Tip

For an outrageously indulgent dessert, serve with a glossy chocolate sauce (p.46).

Opposite: Chocolate and Raspberry Torte.

Creamy Chocolate Rice Pudding

Serves 4-5

1 oz/¼ cup chopped mixed nuts
1 oz/2 tablespoons white rice
1 tablespoon cocoa powder
1 teaspoon ground mixed spice (apple pie spice)
2 oz/⅓ cup sultanas (golden raisins)
1 pint/2½ cups milk
¼ pint/⅔ cup heavy cream
4 oz/4 squares dark chocolate, roughly chopped
Freshly grated nutmeg for sprinkling

Grease a 2 pint/5 cup ovenproof dish lightly. Toast the nuts lightly.

Sprinkle the rice, cocoa powder, spice, and sultanas into the dish. Bring the milk and the cream to the boil, remove from the heat and stir in the chocolate until it has melted. Pour over the rice mixture, stirring gently. Sprinkle the surface with nutmeg.

Bake in a preheated oven at 300°F for 1 hour. Stir gently and sprinkle with the nuts. Return to the oven for a further 30–60 minutes until turning golden. Serve hot.

Above: Creamy Chocolate Rice Pudding being prepared.

Steamed Chocolate Bread Pudding with Apple and Raisin Topping

Serves 5-6

Topping: 2 oz/¾ cup dried apple chunks, roughly chopped
1 oz/1½ tablespoons dark brown sugar
1 oz/3 tablespoons raisins
½ oz/1 tablespoon unsalted butter

Pudding: 3 oz/3 squares dark or milk chocolate
3 oz/⅓ cup unsalted butter or margarine
3 oz/⅓ cup superfine sugar
1 egg, separated
2 oz/½ cup self-raising flour
1 teaspoon ground mixed spice (apple pie spice)
1 tablespoon cocoa powder
4 oz/2 cups fresh breadcrumbs
Milk

To make the topping, place the dried apples in a saucepan with the sugar, raisins, butter, and 4 fl oz/½ cup water. Bring to the boil, reduce the heat and simmer gently for 10 minutes. Remove from heat and leave to cool.

Butter a 2 pint/5 cup pudding or charlotte mold lightly and spoon the apple mixture into the base. To make the pudding, chop the chocolate into small pieces. Cream together the butter or margarine and sugar until pale and creamy. Beat in the egg yolk, then the chopped chocolate. Sift the flour, spice, and cocoa powder into the bowl and fold into the mixture with the breadcrumbs. Add enough milk to make a soft dropping consistency.

Beat the egg white in a separate bowl until stiff, then fold into the chocolate mixture. Spoon into the prepared mold and level the surface. Cover with a double thickness of baking parchment and a layer of foil, securing under the rim. Place in a steamer set over a pan of simmering water. Alternatively, rest on an upturned saucer in a large saucepan. Add enough boiling water to come half-way up the sides of the mold, then cover the pan. Steam for about 2 hours until the pudding feels firm. Invert on a serving plate and serve with cream.

Cook's Tip

Do not forget to check the water level frequently, refill with boiling water if necessary.

Sticky Blueberry Upside-Down Cake

Serves 4

6 oz/1 cup blueberries
9 oz/9 squares dark chocolate
4 oz/½ cup unsalted butter
2 eggs
3 oz/½ cup light brown sugar
1 teaspoon vanilla extract
3 oz/¾ cup self-raising flour
3 tablespoons clear honey or light corn syrup

Grease and line the base of an 8 inch round shallow baking pan. Scatter with the blueberries.

Chop 4 oz/4 squares of the chocolate roughly. Break the remaining chocolate into pieces and place in a heat-proof bowl over a pan of simmering water. Add the butter and leave to simmer until the mixture has melted. Leave to cool slightly.

Beat together the eggs, sugar, and vanilla extract. Beat in the chocolate mixture, then fold in the flour and the chopped chocolate. Spoon into the prepared dish and bake in a preheated oven at 375°F for about 50–60 minutes until firm. Invert on a flat serving dish, peel away the lining paper and drizzle with the honey or syrup. Serve warm with cream or ice cream.

Variation

Substitute 3 small ripe pears for the blueberries. Peel, quarter, and core them, and arrange them in the base of the dish.

Chocolate and Orange Brulées

Serves 4

1 orange
¾ pint/2 cups heavy cream
6 oz/6 squares dark chocolate, roughly chopped
4 egg yolks
2 oz/¼ cup superfine sugar
Confectioners' sugar for dusting

Using a citrus zester, pare strips of rind from the orange. (Alternatively, grate the orange rind.) Place half the rind in a saucepan with the cream and chocolate, and heat gently, stirring until completely smooth.

Place the egg yolks and superfine sugar in a bowl and whisk lightly. Pour the chocolate mixture over the yolks gradually, whisking until smooth. Turn into four individual ramekins. Place in a roasting pan and pour a ½ inch depth of boiling water into the pan. Cover with foil and bake in a preheated oven at 400°F for about 15 minutes or until beginning to set. Drain off the water.

Sprinkle confectioners' sugar over the ramekins in an even layer. Cook the brulées under a preheated broiler for several minutes until the sugar begins to caramelize. Scatter with the reserved orange rind and serve dusted with confectioners' sugar.

Variation

Omit the orange rind and add 2 teaspoons instant coffee granules to the egg yolks with the chocolate.

Opposite: Sticky Blueberry Upside-Down Cake.

Chocolate Meringue Pie

Serves 6

Pastry:

5 oz/1¼ cups all-purpose flour
1 oz/¼ cup cocoa powder
3 oz/⅓ cup unsalted butter
2 tablespoons superfine sugar
1 egg yolk

Filling:

6 oz/6 squares dark chocolate
3 oz/¾ cup cornstarch
2 egg yolks
2 oz/¼ cup superfine sugar
1 pint/2½ cups milk

Meringue:

3 egg whites
6 oz/¾ cup superfine sugar

To make the pastry, sift the flour and cocoa powder into a bowl. Cut the butter into small pieces, and rub into the flour with your fingertips until the mixture resembles fine breadcrumbs. Stir in the sugar. Add the egg yolk and enough cold water to bring the mix to a firm dough. Transfer to a floured work surface and knead lightly. Chill for about 30 minutes.

Roll out the pastry and use to line a 9 inch round, loose-based flan pan. Line with baking parchment and baking beans and then bake in a preheated oven at 400°F for 15 minutes. Remove the beans and paper.

To make the filling, break the chocolate into pieces. Mix

Previous page: Left to right, Chocolate Meringue Pie, and Pears with Chocolate and Hazelnuts.

together the cornstarch, egg yolks, sugar, and a little of the milk. Bring the remaining milk to the boil in a small saucepan and pour over the yolk mixture. Return the mixture to the pan, bring to the boil, stirring, and cook until thickened. Remove from the heat and stir in the chocolate until it has melted. Pour into the pastry case and leave to cool.

To make the meringue, beat the egg whites until stiff. Beat in the sugar gradually, a little at a time, and beat well after each addition until the mixture is stiff and glossy. Spoon over the filling and swirl into peaks. Bake for about 5 minutes or until the meringue is turning golden. Serve warm with cream.

Cook's Tip

Watch the meringue closely during cooking as it will color quite suddenly. It looks most appetizing when the tips of the peaks are golden, but the meringue remains almost white.

Almond and Chocolate Pithiviers

Serves 6

2 tablespoons slivered almonds
2 oz/¼ cup unsalted butter, softened
2 tablespoons brandy

2 oz/½ cup ground almonds
2 tablespoons cocoa powder
1 egg
2 oz/2 squares dark chocolate, finely chopped
1 lb puff pastry
Beaten egg for glazing
Confectioners' sugar for dusting

Grease a baking sheet lightly and dampen. Toast the slivered almonds.

Place the butter in a bowl with the brandy and sugar, and beat until light and fluffy. Stir in the ground almonds, cocoa powder, egg, and chopped chocolate.

Roll out the pastry on a lightly floured work surface to a 16x8 inch rectangle. Using a plate as a guide, cut out two circles, each 8 inches in diameter. Transfer one pastry circle to the prepared baking sheet. Brush the rim of the pastry with water and sprinkle the toasted almonds over the center. Spoon the almond filling over the toasted almonds, spreading to a flat cake which comes to 2 inches of the edge of the pastry.

Roll out the remaining pastry circle lightly until slightly larger and lift over the base. Press the edges together to seal. Flute the edges at 1 inch intervals with the back of a knife. Brush the top of the pastry with the beaten egg. Using the tip of a sharp knife, make spiral cuts from the center of the pastry out to the edges to decorate. Bake in a preheated oven at 400°F for about 30 minutes until well-risen and deep golden, covering with foil if the pastry starts to overbrown. Dust with confectioners' sugar and serve warm or cold with cream.

Pears with Chocolate and Hazelnuts

Serves 4

4 ripe pears
2 oz/½ cup hazelnuts
3 oz/3 squares dark chocolate
½ teaspoon ground cinnamon
¼ pint/⅔ cup heavy cream
Confectioners' sugar

Halve the pears and scoop out the cores. Cut a thin slice off each pear so that they sit flat. Place in a large shallow ovenproof dish.

Chop and toast the hazelnuts lightly. Sprinkle half into the cavity of each pear. Chop the chocolate roughly and scatter over the pears with the remaining nuts. Sprinkle with the cinnamon. Fill each cavity with a little cream and then dust each pear with confectioners' sugar.

Cook under a preheated moderate broiler for about 5 minutes until the pears are beginning to color and the cream is bubbling. Serve hot, with any remaining cream.

Cook's Tip

Choose really ripe, juicy pears which will be easier to cut and much fuller in flavor.

Chocolate Walnut Pie

Serves 8-10

Pastry:
6 oz/1½ cups all-purpose flour
1 oz/¼ cup cocoa powder
4 oz/½ cup unsalted butter
2 oz/¼ cup superfine sugar
2 egg yolks

Filling:
6 oz/1 cup light brown sugar
¼ pint/⅔ cup maple syrup
2 oz/¼ cup unsalted butter
½ teaspoon vanilla extract
2 tablespoons cocoa powder
3 eggs
1 tablespoon milk
8 oz/2 cups broken walnuts

pour over the syrup mixture. Sprinkle with the remaining nuts. Bake in a preheated oven at 400°F for 10 minutes, then reduce the oven temperature to 325°F and bake for a further 40–45 minutes until just set. Serve warm or cold with cream.

Cook's Tip

Keep an eye on the pie towards the end of cooking time. Cover it with foil if it starts to overbrown.

To make the pastry, sift the flour and cocoa powder into a bowl. Cut the butter into small pieces, and rub into the flour with your fingertips until the mixture resembles breadcrumbs. Stir in the sugar and the egg yolks with a dash of cold water to make a firm dough. Transfer the dough to a lightly floured surface and knead lightly. Chill for 30 minutes. Roll out the pastry and use to line a 9 inch loose-based flan pan.

To make the filling, place the sugar and syrup in a saucepan and heat gently until the sugar has dissolved. Pour into a bowl and stir in the butter and vanilla extract. Add the cocoa powder, eggs, and milk, and beat until smooth. Sprinkle half the walnuts into the pastry case and

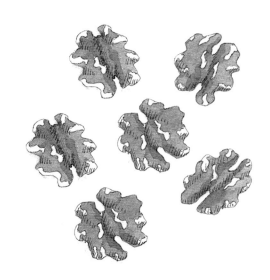

Opposite: Chocolate Walnut Pie.

A special chocolate dessert provides the perfect excuse for combining all of our favorite ingredients in one delicious concoction! Chocolate, cream, and liqueurs are the basis of delicious desserts such as the Chocolate Truffle Slice (p.56), Layered Chocolate Trifle (p.48) or White Chocolate Creams (p.47). There are also classic recipes in this chapter like Profiteroles (this page) with a Glossy Chocolate Sauce, and interesting variations on a Pavlova (p.54) and White Chocolate Roulade (p.58).

Although these recipes require a little time for preparation, most can be made a day in advance, for finishing with cream and other decorations an hour before serving.

Profiteroles with Glossy Chocolate Sauce

Serves 5-6

Pastry: 2½ oz/¼ cup plus 2 tablespoons all-purpose flour
2 oz/¼ cup unsalted butter
2 eggs, lightly beaten

Sauce: 5 oz/5 squares dark chocolate
½ oz/1 tablespoon unsalted butter
2 tablespoons light corn syrup

To Finish: ¼ pint/⅔ cup heavy cream
1 tablespoon confectioners' sugar
Extra confectioners' sugar for dusting

Grease 2 baking sheets lightly and dampen. Sift the flour on to a plate or piece of paper.

Place the butter in a small saucepan with ¼ pint/⅔ cup water. Heat gently until the butter melts; then bring to the boil. Remove from the heat immediately and add the sifted flour. Beat thoroughly until smooth. Return to the heat and cook until the mixture comes away cleanly from the sides of the pan. Leave to cool for 2 minutes.

Beat in the eggs, a little at a time, until the mixture is smooth and glossy. Place in a pastry bag fitted with a large plain tip. Pipe small blobs, about 1 inch in diameter, on to the baking sheets. Bake in a preheated oven at 425°F for 20 minutes until well-risen, crisp and golden. Remove from the oven and make a cut in the side of each bun. Return to the oven for a further 5 minutes for the centers to dry out. Transfer to a wire rack to cool.

Previous page: Left to right, White Chocolate Creams, Profiteroles with Glossy Chocolate Sauce, and Layered Chocolate Trifle.

To make the sauce, break the chocolate into pieces and place in a saucepan with the butter, syrup, and 1 tablespoon cold water. Heat gently over a slow heat, stirring until smooth and glossy.

Whip the cream with the confectioners' sugar until it is just peaking. Spoon or pipe the mixture into the buns and pile them up on a serving plate. Dust with confectioners' sugar and pour over a little chocolate sauce. Serve with any remaining sauce.

Variation

For a special dessert, add a splash of brandy or orange-flavored liqueur to the cream when whipping.

White Chocolate Creams

Serves 6

2 small ripe bananas
1 tablespoon lemon juice
6 oz/6 squares white chocolate
½ pint/1¼ cups milk
½ pint/1¼ cups heavy cream
4 egg yolks
1 oz/3 tablespoons superfine sugar
1 teaspoon cornstarch
2 tablespoons Cointreau or orange-flavored liqueur

To Decorate:
3 oz/3 squares dark or milk chocolate
2 tablespoons heavy cream
Fresh mint leaves
Chocolate mint leaves (p.6), optional
Confectioners' sugar for dusting

Peel the bananas and slice thinly. Toss with the lemon juice and spoon into six tall stemmed glasses. Break the chocolate into small pieces.

Put the milk and cream into a saucepan and heat gently. Beat together the egg yolks, sugar, and cornstarch in a bowl. Pour the hot milk and cream over the egg yolk mixture, stirring. Return to the saucepan and cook gently until thick enough to coat the back of a wooden spoon. Remove from the heat and stir in the white chocolate until it has melted; then add the liqueur. Leave to cool slightly; then spoon over the bananas in the glasses. Leave to cool.

To decorate, break the chocolate into pieces and melt with the cream in a heatproof bowl over a pan of simmering water. Spoon over the desserts, swirling to the edges of the glasses. Decorate with fresh mint leaves and chocolate mint leaves, if liked. Dust lightly with confectioners' sugar.

Variation

Use dark or milk chocolate instead of the white chocolate, and add 2 teaspoons cocoa powder. White or dark rum can be added instead of the orange-flavored liqueur.

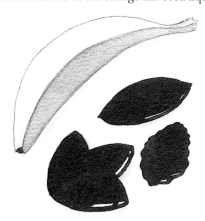

Rich Chocolate Bavarois

Serves 6

8 oz/8 squares dark chocolate
½ oz/1 envelope powdered gelatin
3 egg yolks
1½ oz/3 tablespoons superfine sugar
1 teaspoon cornstarch
½ pint/1¼ cups milk
1 egg white
½ pint/1¼ cups heavy cream

To Serve:

Raspberries
Redcurrants
Blackcurrants
Mint leaves
Confectioners' sugar for dusting

Break the chocolate into pieces. Sprinkle the gelatin over 3 tablespoons water in a small bowl. Whisk the egg yolks with ½ oz/1 tablespoon of the sugar and the cornstarch. Bring the milk to the boil in a saucepan and pour over the egg yolk mixture, stirring. Return the mixture to the pan and heat gently, stirring continuously until it is slightly thickened. Remove from the heat and stir in the gelatin, then the chocolate until smooth. Leave the custard to cool.

Beat the egg white until stiff; then beat in the remaining sugar gradually. Whip the cream until it is just peaking. Using a large metal spoon, fold the cream into the chocolate mixture carefully; then fold in the egg white. Spoon into a wetted 2 pint/5 cup jelly mold or six individual molds and chill until just set.

To serve the bavarois, dip the mold into a bowl of very hot water for several seconds and then invert on a serving plate, shaking the mold to release the bavarois. Surround with raspberries, redcurrants, and blackcurrants then decorate with mint leaves. Dust the fruits with confectioners' sugar.

Cook's Tip

Dip the mold very cautiously when releasing the bavarois, returning the mold to the water in short bursts if necessary. If the mold is steeped for too long, the edges of the bavarois will melt and look very messy.

Layered Chocolate Trifle

Serves 6-8

8 oz almond macaroons
12 oz ripe apricots
3 tablespoons Tia Maria or brandy
3 oz/3 squares dark chocolate
1 egg yolk
2 teaspoons cornstarch
1 tablespoon superfine sugar
½ pint/1¼ cups milk

Topping:

3 tablespoons Tia Maria
3 tablespoons strong dark coffee
4 tablespoons confectioners' sugar
½ pint/1¼ cups heavy cream
Cocoa powder for dusting
Piped chocolate pieces to decorate (p.7)

Place the cookies in a glass serving dish. Halve and remove the pits from the apricots. Cut them into wedges and scatter over the cookies. Spoon over the liqueur or brandy.

Break the chocolate into pieces. Mix the egg yolk, cornstarch, sugar, and a dash of the milk in a bowl. Bring the remaining milk to the boil and pour over the egg yolk mixture, whisking well; then return it to the saucepan. Cook, stirring, until thickened. Remove from the heat and stir in the chocolate until it has melted. Leave to cool, then pour the custard over the apricots and level the surface. Leave to cool completely.

To make the topping, place the Tia Maria, coffee, confectioners' sugar, and cream in a bowl and beat until the mixture forms soft peaks. Spoon over the chocolate custard. Dust lightly with cocoa powder and finish with piped chocolate decorations.

Cook's Tip

Make sure the apricots are the soft, dessert variety. If preferred, used canned apricots, or substitute a mixture of soft fruits.

Petit Pots au Chocolat

Serves 6	8 oz/8 squares dark chocolate
	½ pint/1¼ cups milk
	½ pint/1¼ cups light cream
	1 teaspoon vanilla extract
	1 egg
	3 egg yolks
	1 oz/2½ tablespoons superfine sugar
To Decorate:	Whipped cream
	Cocoa powder for dusting

Break the chocolate into pieces. Place the milk, cream, and vanilla extract in a saucepan and bring just to the boil. Stir in the chocolate until it has melted.

Mix together the egg, egg yolks, and sugar in a large bowl. Beat in the chocolate mixture. Strain into six small ramekins or small ovenproof cups. Stand the containers in a roasting pan, then pour a ¾ inch depth of water into the pan. Cover with foil and bake in a preheated oven at 300°F for 50–60 minutes until the custard feels lightly set. Remove from the oven and leave to cool, then chill until ready to serve. Top each serving with lightly whipped cream and dust with cocoa powder.

Variation

For a mildly spiced flavor, add ½ teaspoon ground cinnamon when mixing the eggs. Alternatively, try adding the finely grated rind of ½ orange.

Next page: Left to right, Petit Pots au Chocolat and Rich Chocolate Bavarois.

Chocolate Swirled Cheesecake

Serves 10-12

Base:

6 oz graham crackers
3 oz/⅓ cup unsalted butter
1 oz/2 tablespoons light brown sugar

Filling:

4 oz/4 squares dark chocolate
1 lb 2 oz/2¼ cups cream cheese
3 oz/½ cup light brown sugar
½ oz/2 tablespoons all-purpose flour
3 eggs
2 tablespoons cocoa powder
1 oz/3 tablespoons raisins
1 teaspoon vanilla extract

Grease and line an 8 inch spring form cake pan. Place the crackers in a thick plastic bag and crush with a rolling pin. Melt the butter in a saucepan. Add the crushed crackers and sugar, and stir until evenly combined. Spoon into the prepared pan and spread evenly over the base. Pack down lightly with the back of the spoon.

To make the filling, break the chocolate into pieces and melt in a heatproof bowl over a saucepan of simmering water. Put the cream cheese in a bowl and beat with the sugar until smooth. Beat in the flour and eggs. Spoon a third of the mixture into a separate bowl and beat in the melted chocolate and cocoa powder. Beat the raisins and vanilla extract into the mixture.

Place alternate spoonfuls of the chocolate and vanilla-flavored mixture in the pan. Using a skewer, swirl the two mixtures together lightly to give a marbled effect. Bake in a preheated oven at 325°F for about 1 hour, then turn off

the oven and leave the cheesecake to cool in the oven for a further 1 hour. Serve warm or chilled with cream.

Cook's Tip

This delicious cheesecake is very rich, so serve small portions. If preferred, substitute roughly chopped, toasted hazelnuts, or walnuts for the raisins.

Chocolate Coconut Torte

Serves 10-12

Filling:

14 oz/14 squares white chocolate
2 eggs, separated
1¼ pints/3 cups heavy cream
4 oz/4 squares dark chocolate
3 tablespoons Cointreau or orange-flavored liqueur

Base:

8oz coconut cookies
4 oz/½ cup unsalted butter

Grease the base and sides of a 9 inch round loose-based cake pan. Line with baking parchment, but do not grease the paper.

Break the white chocolate into pieces and melt in a heatproof bowl with the egg yolks and 4 tablespoons of the cream. Melt the dark chocolate in a separate bowl with the liqueur. Whip ¼ pint/⅔ cup of the cream lightly and mix with the dark chocolate. Place in a pastry bag fitted with a ½ inch plain tip and pipe dots, about ¾ inch in diameter, on to the base of the prepared pan. Reserve the remainder and chill the pan.

Whip the remaining cream and fold in the white chocolate mixture. Spoon over the dark chocolate in the pan and level the surface. Pipe the remaining dark chocolate in the bag immediately into the white chocolate, to create spots of color when the torte is sliced.

To make the base, place the cookies in a strong plastic bag and crush finely with a rolling pin. Melt the butter in a saucepan and stir in the crushed cookies until evenly coated. Scatter over the chocolate mixture in the pan and press down lightly. Chill for several hours or overnight.

To serve, invert the torte on a serving plate and peel away the lining paper. Serve very small slices.

Cook's Tip

Both chocolate mixtures set firm quite soon so you will need to work quickly when assembling the torte. It will help slightly to use the cream at room temperature.

Mud Pie

Serves 8

Pastry:
6 oz/1½ cups all-purpose flour
4 oz/½ cup unsalted butter
1 oz/2 tablespoons light brown sugar
2 teaspoons instant coffee powder

Filling:
1½ teaspoons powdered gelatin
7 oz/7 squares dark chocolate
3 oz/½ cup light brown sugar
2 tablespoons cornstarch
2 egg yolks
½ pint/1¼ cups milk
1 tablespoon instant coffee powder
¾ pint/2 cups heavy cream
Grated chocolate or chocolate chips to decorate
Cocoa powder for dusting

To make the pastry, sift the flour into a bowl. Cut the butter into small pieces, and rub into the flour with your fingertips until the mixture begins to bind together. Stir in the sugar and coffee powder, and mix to a dough.

Grease an 8 inch loose-based flan pan lightly. Press the pastry dough around the base and sides of the pan until evenly lined. Bake in a preheated oven at 350°F for about 20 minutes; then leave to cool.

To make the filling, sprinkle the gelatin over 2 tablespoons water in a small bowl. Leave to soften. Break the chocolate into pieces. Beat the sugar, cornstarch, and egg yolks together. Place the milk in a saucepan with the coffee powder. Bring just to the boil; then pour over the egg yolk mixture. Return to the saucepan and cook, stirring, until thickened. Stir in the softened gelatin. When this has dissolved, add the chocolate and stir until smooth and melted. Stir in ½ pint/1¼ cups of the cream and pour into the prepared shell. Cover and chill until lightly set.

Whip the remaining cream very lightly and swirl over the filling. Decorate with grated chocolate or chocolate chips and serve dusted with cocoa powder.

Cook's Tip

The rich, gooey filling of this delicious pie will have a slightly firmer texture if left to set overnight. For a lighter, more everyday version, use a shortcrust (plain) pastry shell and replace the cream in the filling with additional milk.

Chocolate Chip Pavlova

Serves 8-10

5 egg whites
11 oz/scant 1½ cups superfine sugar
3 oz/¾ cup dark or milk chocolate chips
2 teaspoons white wine vinegar
2 teaspoons cornstarch

To Decorate:

8 oz/1½ cups strawberries
4 oz/4 squares dark chocolate
½ pint/1¼ cups heavy cream
1 tablespoon confectioners' sugar

Grease a large baking sheet lightly and line with non-stick baking parchment. Draw an 8½ inch circle on the paper, using a plate as a guide.

Opposite: Chocolate Chip Pavlova.

Place the egg whites in a large, clean bowl and beat until stiff. Beat in the superfine sugar gradually, a table-spoonful at a time, until the mixture is very thick and glossy, ensuring that the mixture is beaten well between each addition. Fold in the chocolate chips lightly, then the vinegar and cornstarch.

Spoon the meringue on to the prepared baking sheet and spread to the edge of the marked circle, swirling the mixture attractively into soft peaks. Bake in a preheated oven at 300°F for 5 minutes, then reduce the oven temperature to 250°F and bake for a further 1 hour or until the meringue is crisp. Leave to cool on the baking sheet.

To decorate, dip the strawberries in 2 oz/2 squares of the melted chocolate (p.71). Use the remaining chocolate to make chocolate rose leaves (p.6).

Beat the cream with the confectioners' sugar until it is peaking. Transfer the meringue to a serving plate and swirl with the cream. Scatter the dipped strawberries over the surface and decorate with the chocolate leaves.

Chocolate Truffle Slice

Serves 10-12

3 oz ginger snap cookies
Piece of candied ginger in syrup,
plus 4 tablespoons of juices from the jar
1 lb dark chocolate
2 oz/¼ cup unsalted butter
1 pint/2½ cups heavy cream
4 tablespoons brandy

To Finish:

Crushed cookies
Cocoa powder
Confectioners' sugar

Put the cookies in a strong plastic bag and crush firmly with a rolling pin. Grease and line only the sides of a 9 inch spring form pan before scattering the cookies over the base.

Chop the candied ginger finely. Break the chocolate into pieces and place it in a heavy-based saucepan with the butter, chopped ginger, and the juices. Cook over a very gentle heat until the butter and chocolate have melted. Stir until smooth.

Beat the cream with the brandy until it begins to thicken. Place the chocolate mixture in a separate bowl and fold in the cream gradually until evenly combined. Spoon over the cookies in the pan and level the surface. Cover and chill for several hours or overnight.

To serve, transfer the cake to a serving plate and peel away the lining paper. Dust generously with the crushed cookies, confectioners' sugar, and the cocoa powder, and serve in small slices.

Chocolate Mousse Cups

Serves 6

Cups:	8 oz/8 squares dark chocolate
	1 small orange
Mousse:	4 oz/4 squares dark chocolate
	4 eggs, separated

To Decorate: Small selection of fresh fruits, such as strawberries, redcurrants, raspberries, kiwi fruit, and grapes

To make the cups, break the chocolate into pieces and melt in a heatproof bowl over a saucepan of simmering water. Cut a double-thickness circle of foil, about 7 inches in diameter, and wrap around a whole orange, letting the edges open out slightly to make a cup shape. Remove from the orange and press the foil shell on to the work surface to make a flat base. Make five more shells in the same way.

Spoon a little of the melted chocolate into one of the foil shells. Smooth up the sides with the back of a teaspoon, giving the edges an uneven, rough edge. Repeat on the remaining cups. Chill the cups until set firmly. Peel away the foil from each cup carefully, starting around the top edges, and peeling down to the base. Place the shells on a small tray or baking sheet.

To make the mousse, break the chocolate into pieces and melt with 2 tablespoons boiling water in a heatproof bowl over a saucepan of simmering water. Add the yolks to the melted chocolate and stir gently. Beat the egg whites in a large bowl until stiff. Using a large metal spoon, fold a

Left: Chocolate Truffle Slice.

quarter into the chocolate mixture; then fold in the remainder carefully.

Spoon the mousse into the chocolate shells and leave for several hours until set. Arrange the fruits over the shells to decorate before serving.

Cook's Tip

The mousse filling is one of the simplest and most delicious you can make. Serve it in small glasses with a swirl of cream as a quick and easy dessert.

White Chocolate Roulade

Serves 8

Roulade:
5 oz/5 squares white chocolate
4 eggs, separated
3 oz/⅓ cup superfine sugar
Extra superfine sugar for sprinkling

To Finish:
1 lb soft fruits such as strawberries, raspberries, blackcurrants, and redcurrants
2½ fl oz/5 tablespoons kirsch
2 tablespoons superfine sugar
¼ pint/⅔ cup crème fraîche

Grease and line a 13x9 inch jelly roll pan with greased non-stick baking parchment. Break the chocolate into pieces and melt in a heatproof bowl over a saucepan of simmering water.

Whisk the egg yolks in a bowl with the sugar. Beat in the melted chocolate and 1 tablespoon hot water. Beat the egg whites until stiff. Using a large metal spoon, fold a quarter of the egg whites carefully into the chocolate

mixture; then fold in the remainder. Spoon into the prepared pan and ease the mixture gently into the corners. Bake in a preheated oven at 350°F for 20-25 minutes until risen and just firm to the touch.

Sprinkle a clean sheet of non-stick baking parchment with superfine sugar. Invert the cake on the paper and peel away the lining paper. Cover with a damp dish towel and leave to cool.

Halve any large strawberries and mix in a bowl with 4 tablespoons of the kirsch and 1 tablespoon of the sugar. Leave until ready to serve, stirring occasionally.

Stir the remaining kirsch and sugar into the crème fraîche and spread over the roulade. Roll up the roulade starting from a short end, pulling up the paper underneath to help it to roll easily. Transfer to a serving plate and dust with a little extra sugar. Transfer the fruits to a serving bowl. Serve the roulade with spoonfuls of fruit.

Cook's Tip

Crème fraîche makes a lovely contrast with the sweetness of the chocolate. Lightly whipped heavy cream can be used instead if preferred.

Left: White Chocolate Roulade served with soft fruits.

Rich in cream and real chocolate, there is nothing to beat the delicious flavor of home-made ice cream. Using beaten eggs and cream, the following recipes are simple to follow and can, of course, be made two to three weeks in advance.

For special occasion desserts there are some frozen gâteaus like the Chocolate Cherry Meringue (p.67), White Chocolate and Coffee Torte (p.62) and Chocolate Macaroon Tortoni (p.66). All these ease the burden of last-minute preparation, and simply need to be transferred to the refrigerator for a short time before serving to make slicing or scooping easier.

Iced Chocolate Mousse

Serves 6

5 oz/5 squares dark chocolate
2 oz/½ cup cocoa powder
2 tablespoons light corn syrup
2 tablespoons brandy
4 eggs
2 egg yolks
¼ pint/⅝ cup heavy cream
Feathered chocolate pieces (p.7) to decorate

Break the chocolate into pieces and melt in a heatproof bowl over a saucepan of simmering water. Add the cocoa powder, corn syrup, and the brandy, then stir until the mixture is smooth.

Place the eggs and extra egg yolks in a large bowl and beat with an electric mixer until thick and pale. Whip the cream in a separate bowl until it is just peaking.

Pour the chocolate mixture over the beaten eggs, then fold in gently using a large metal spoon. Fold in the cream. Spoon the mixture into a freezer container and freeze overnight until firm.

Using an ice cream scoop, take small balls of the ice cream and arrange in serving glasses. Serve decorated with feathered chocolate pieces.

Variation
For a dinner party dessert, serve the iced chocolate mousse in pretty chocolate shells (p.57).

Opposite: Top, Iced Chocolate Mousse, bottom, Chocolate Macaroon Tortoni (p.66).

White Chocolate and Coffee Torte

Serves 8-10   ½ pint/1¼ cups strong black coffee
4 tablespoons Tia Maria or Kahlua
12 oz/12 squares white chocolate
1 pint/2½ cups heavy cream
2 oz/½ cup chocolate-covered coffee beans
1 tablespoon confectioners' sugar
2 packets sponge fingers (lady-fingers)

To Decorate: Run-out chocolate leaves (p.7)
Extra chocolate-covered coffee beans
Cocoa powder for dusting

Mix the coffee with the Tia Maria or Kahlua in a bowl. Break the chocolate into pieces and place in a heavy-based saucepan with ½ pint/1¼ cups of the cream. Cook very gently, stirring frequently until the chocolate has melted and the mixture is smooth. Remove from the heat and pour into a bowl. Stir in the remaining cream and leave to cool.

Place the chocolate-covered coffee beans in a strong plastic bag and crush with a rolling pin until fairly finely ground. Dip the sponge fingers briefly in the coffee liquid so that a little is absorbed but the cookies do not turn soggy. Transfer to a plate. When all the cookies have been dipped, add any remaining liquid to the cream and whip until mixture is softly peaking.

Spoon a third of the cream into the base of a 9 inch round spring form pan. Arrange half the sponge fingers over the cream, so that they are evenly layered. Scatter half the chocolate-covered coffee beans on top. Spread half the remaining cream over the sponge fingers and then cover

with the remaining sponge fingers. Scatter the remaining coffee beans on top. Spoon the remaining cream into the pan and spread to the edges, swirl the surface attractively. Cover the pan and freeze overnight.

To serve, loosen the edges of the pan with a knife and then remove the sides of the pan. Slide a fish spatula under the cake and transfer to a flat serving plate. Chill for 1–2 hours before serving partially frozen, or leave to thaw completely. Decorate with the chocolate leaves and coffee beans, and serve dusted with cocoa powder.

Cook's Tip

Chocolate-covered coffee beans are available from some confectioners and gourmet shops. If you cannot find any, substitute the same quantity of dark chocolate, finely chopped.

Left: White Chocolate and Coffee Torte.

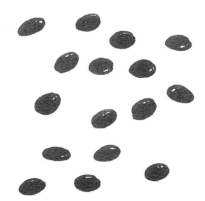

Chunky Chocolate Fudge Ice Cream

Serves 6-8

6 oz/6 squares dark chocolate
3 oz creamy fudge
6 eggs, separated
4 oz/½ cup superfine sugar
½ pint/1¼ cups heavy cream

To Serve: 1 oz/¼ cup broken walnuts or pecan nuts, toasted
Dessert cookies

Break the chocolate into pieces and melt in a heatproof bowl over a saucepan of simmering water. Cut the fudge into small chunks.

Beat the egg whites in a large bowl until stiff. Beat in the sugar gradually, a teaspoonful at a time, until the mixture is stiff and glossy.

Beat the egg yolks in a separate bowl, until pale. Beat in the melted chocolate gradually. Whip the cream until it is just peaking; then fold it into the egg yolk mixture with the chunks of fudge. Using a large metal spoon; fold a quarter of the egg white into the chocolate mixture to lighten it; then fold in the remainder carefully. Spoon into a freezer container and freeze overnight until firm.

To serve, scoop the ice cream into glass serving dishes and scatter with toasted nuts. Serve with dessert cookies.

Cook's Tip

This makes an ice cream with a really creamy texture, perfect for serving straight from the freezer. If liked, serve with a rich chocolate sauce like the one on page 31.

Chocolate Ripple Ice

Serves 4

3 oz/3 squares dark chocolate
9 oz/generous 1 cup mascarpone cheese
2 eggs, separated
1 oz/2 tablespoons superfine sugar
1 teaspoon vanilla extract
Dessert cookies to serve

Break the chocolate into pieces and melt in a heatproof bowl over a saucepan of simmering water.

Beat the mascarpone cheese in a bowl with the egg yolks and sugar until very smooth and creamy. Spoon half the mixture into a separate bowl and beat in the melted chocolate. Beat the vanilla into the remaining mixture.

Beat the egg whites in a separate bowl until stiff. Using a metal spoon, fold half the egg white into the chocolate mixture and half into the vanilla mixture. Alternate spoonfuls of the two mixtures into a freezer container. Using a metal skewer, swirl the two mixtures together roughly. Freeze overnight until firm.

To serve, leave the ice cream at room temperature for 15 minutes; then scoop into serving glasses. Serve with dessert cookies.

Opposite: Frozen delights, left to right,
Chunky Chocolate Fudge Ice Cream and Chocolate Ripple Ice.

Chocolate Macaroon Tortoni

Serves 8

6 oz/1½ cups prunes, roughly chopped
2 tablespoons brandy
6 oz/6 squares dark chocolate
¾ pint/2 cups heavy cream
1 oz/3 tablespoons confectioners' sugar
8 oz macaroons or amaretto cookies
White chocolate rose leaves (p.6) to decorate

Place the prunes in a bowl with the brandy. Cover and leave to soak while preparing the ice cream.

Break the chocolate into pieces and place in a heatproof bowl over a saucepan of simmering water. Add ¼ pint/ ⅔ cup of the cream and leave until melted. Remove from the heat and stir until smooth.

Whip the remaining cream lightly in a bowl with the confectioners' sugar. Stir in the melted chocolate mixture. Spoon into a freezer container and freeze for 2–3 hours until partially frozen.

Place the cookies in a thick plastic bag and beat with a rolling pin until finely crushed. Remove the ice cream from the freezer and mash lightly until broken up. Stir in half the crushed cookies.

Spoon a third of the mixture into a 2 lb loaf pan and scatter with half the prune mixture. Cover with half the remaining ice cream and then the remaining prune mixture. Finally cover with the remaining ice cream mixture and level the surface. Return to the freezer for several hours or overnight until firm.

Dip the pan briefly into hot water; then invert the ice cream on a serving plate. Press the reserved cookies around the sides. Decorate with chocolate leaves and serve cut into slices.

Variation

Use soft dried apricots or dates instead of the prunes. Use ginger wine or sherry instead of the brandy.

Chocolate Cherry Meringue

Serves 10

Meringue:

4 egg whites
8 oz/1 cup superfine sugar
3 oz/½ cup dark or milk chocolate chips

Filling and Decoration:

Two 14 oz cans pitted black cherries, drained
3 tablespoons kirsch
1 pint/2½ cups heavy cream
1 oz/3 tablespoons confectioners' sugar
4 oz/4 squares milk chocolate, finely grated
2 oz/2 squares dark chocolate
Small bunch of fresh cherries

Draw three 9 inch circles on non-stick baking parchment, using a plate as a guide. Place these on three baking sheets.

To make the meringue, beat the egg whites until stiff. Beat in the sugar gradually, a tablespoonful at a time, beat well after each addition, until the mixture is stiff and glossy. Fold in the chocolate chips. Divide the mixture between the three circles, spreading to the edges with a palette knife. Bake in a preheated oven at 275°F for about 1 hour until crisp, rotating the baking sheets on the shelves half-way through cooking. Remove from the oven, peel off the lining paper and leave to cool.

Chop the canned cherries roughly and mix with the kirsch. Whip the cream with the confectioners' sugar and grated milk chocolate until it is only just holding its shape.

Place a meringue layer on a baking sheet or freezer-proof serving plate. Spread with a little of the cream and scatter half the cherries on top. Cover this with another meringue layer and more cream. Scatter the remaining cherries on top. Cover with the remaining meringue layer. Using a spatula, spread the remaining cream over the top and sides of the gâteau, smoothing it down as evenly as possible. Freeze until firm.

To serve, remove the meringue from the freezer and transfer to a flat serving plate if frozen on a baking sheet. Use the dark chocolate and fresh cherries to make dipped fruits (p.7). Leave the meringue to thaw at room temperature for at least 1 hour; then serve decorated with the dipped cherries.

Chocolate Fruit Bombes

Serves 6

Ice Cream:
5 oz/5 squares dark chocolate
½ pint/1¼ cups milk
3 egg yolks
1 teaspoon vanilla extract
2 teaspoons cornstarch
2 oz/¼ cup superfine sugar
½ pint/1¼ cups heavy cream

To Finish:
1 pint/2½ cups good quality bought sorbet
such as mango, orange, strawberry, or another soft fruit
3 oz/3 squares dark or milk chocolate
½ oz/1 tablespoon butter
Appropriate fruits to decorate
Sprigs of fresh mint

To make the ice cream, break the chocolate into pieces and place in a saucepan with the milk. Heat gently until the chocolate melts. Bring to the boil, then remove from the heat and leave to cool slightly. Beat the egg yolks, vanilla extract, cornstarch, and the sugar together until creamy. Blend in the chocolate mixture gradually. Strain the mixture back into the saucepan and cook over a gentle heat, stir continuously until slightly thickened. Remove from the heat and pour into a bowl. Leave the custard to cool completely.

Whisk the cream gradually into the cooled custard, then spoon the mixture into a freezer container and freeze overnight until firm.

Place six individual pudding molds in the freezer to chill. Remove the ice cream from the freezer and leave at room temperature for 20–30 minutes until softened enough to scoop. Spread the softened ice cream around the base and sides of the molds in an even layer, leaving a large cavity in the center. Return to the freezer for at least 1 hour or until firm.

Leave the sorbet at room temperature until slightly softened; then pack it into the center of each mold, making sure that the surface of each one is level. Return to the freezer for a further 1 hour or until firm.

To decorate the ice cream bombes, dip each mold very briefly in hot water until just loosened; then tap out on to serving plates. Return these to the freezer while melting the chocolate.

Break up the chocolate and melt in a heatproof bowl with the butter over a saucepan of simmering water. Place in a pastry bag fitted with a writing tip. (Alternatively, use a paper pastry bag and snip off the tip.) Drizzle random lines of chocolate over the ice cream. Serve decorated with fresh fruits and sprigs of mint.

Cook's Tip

Although these prettily molded ice creams take a little time to prepare, they can be made several days in advance. The chocolate can be piped onto the unmolded ice cream and returned to the freezer in a rigid container. Leave the bombes at room temperature for 10 minutes before serving.

Opposite: Chocolate Fruit Bombes.

Chocolate Sorbet

Serves 6

1 teaspoon powdered gelatin
6 oz/¾ cup granulated sugar
7 oz/7 squares dark chocolate
¼ pint/⅔ cup light cream
2 egg yolks
1 teaspoon vanilla extract
Mint leaves to decorate

Sprinkle the gelatin over 2 tablespoons water in a small bowl. Leave to soften. Place the sugar in a heavy-based saucepan with 1 pint/2½ cups water. Heat gently, stirring, until the sugar has completely dissolved. Bring to the boil and boil for 5 minutes until it is syrupy. Remove from the heat and cool for 3 minutes. Stir in the gelatin until it is dissolved; then leave to cool completely.

Break the chocolate into pieces and place in a heatproof bowl with the cream, egg yolks, and vanilla extract. Rest the bowl over a pan of simmering water and leave until the chocolate has melted. Stir the mixture frequently until it is completely smooth. Remove from the heat and pour in the sugar syrup, stirring well.

Scoop the mixture into a freezer container and freeze for 2–3 hours until partially frozen. Remove from the freezer and mash lightly. Beat with an electric mixer until smooth. Re-freeze the sorbet until completely firm. Serve scooped into glasses, decorated with mint leaves.

Cook's Tip
If you have the time, re-freeze the beaten sorbet partially for a second time and then beat again before freezing until firm. This will give an even smoother result.